Twisted Tales
Two One-Act Plays

Café Perdu
Dark Tales
by
Melissa Collin

Lost and Found
A Dark Comedy
by
Ashley Burgoyne

With **Isolation Stories**

Copyright © Ashley Burgoyne

Copyright © Melissa Collin

First Edition published in 2020

The right of Ashley Burgoyne and Melissa Collin to be identified as the authors of this work has been asserted by them in accordance with the Copyright, Designs and Patents Act 1988

All rights whatsoever in these plays are strictly reserved and applications for permission to perform them, etc., must be made in advance, before rehearsals begin, direct to the authors at ashleyburgoynewriter@gmail.com

Any incidental music, including the arrangements of 'Oranges and Lemons' in Café Perdu, are also available from the above email address.

ISBN: 9798693946255

No one shall make any changes in this title for the purpose of production. No part of this book may be reproduced, stored in a retrieval system, or transmitted in any form, by any means, now known or yet to be invented, including mechanical, electronic, photocopying, recording, videotaping, or otherwise, without the prior written permission of the authors. No one shall upload this title, or part of this title, to any social media websites.

ashleyburgoyne.wixsite.com/writerandcomposer

seaislighterthanthesky.blogspot.co.uk

newfrontierstheatre.wixsite.com/newfrontiers

Café Perdu
Dark Tales
by
Melissa Collin

Cast

Introduction
John & Linda (*Bartenders at the Café*)

Scene 1
Tony & Denise (*Work colleagues*)

Scene 2
Adrian & Grace (*Brother and sister*)

Interlude
John & Linda

Scene 3
Simon & Angie (*Long-standing friends and former partners*)

Scene 4
John & Linda

The actors can be from a wide age range, but should be a similar age to each other, and of the age to have children from late teens to early twenties.

Introduction

Music fades and lights up on a rather dingy café bar. It has seen better days but is open from very early to very late. It is frequented by people who need somewhere to go to at all times of the day.
John enters from SL, carrying a teapot. Linda enters from SR carrying cups and saucers/mugs. They are dressed for bar work in black trousers and white shirts. Linda wears an apron wrapped around her waist in which she keeps a notepad.

They approach the table, centre stage. On the table is a menu and a vase containing flowers. They place the props on the table and adjust the chairs. Linda adjusts the teapot slightly.

LINDA   There. I think we're ready for them. *(She takes a notepad from her apron and a pen from her hair)*

The refrain from 'Oranges and Lemons' sounds from somewhere. They look upwards, look at each other, then look out at the audience.

JOHN   You'd better open the door.

Linda goes off SR, John SL. Lights down. They will change costumes to daytime business clothes.

Scene 1

Lights up. It is morning. A man is sitting at one of the tables, dressed for the office. A teapot and two cups and saucers are in front of him. He seems bored and is scrolling through his phone. He stands, as a woman in a slightly quirkier attempt at business clothes rushes in at great speed from SR, unfastening her coat as she moves towards him.

DENISE *(breathlessly)* Sorry… so sorry. I'm late, I know, but I…

TONY *(standing and looking at his watch, cuts her off)* But you're not late. In fact you're three minutes early.

DENISE Really? Well, I usually am late, so I always think it best to apologise anyway, so that I'm not seen as so very rude, when really my intention is never to offend…

TONY *(trying again)*… but you're not…

DENISE … and I was up so early. The cat, you know? She has her routines, which usually involve waking me at some God-awful early time, when even the larks are still sending home the Zs. I always think I'd make a good milkman, or a postman. Woman, I mean….

TONY *(still trying to cut her off)* … shall we just both accept that you are not late, I am not offended, and would not have been even if you had been late?

DENISE *(still talking over him)* Of course it was such a beautiful morning that it was almost a pleasure to be up. The rosy dawn, the birdsong. The first cup of tea. I had no milk, though. Of course, if I was a milkman… woman… that wouldn't be a problem, would it?

TONY *(firmly)* Would you like to take off your coat? *(Goes around behind her to help)*

DENISE *(finally shutting up)* Oh. Yes. Thank you. *(A little flustered)* I don't think any man apart from my father has ever helped me off with my coat.

TONY Well, it costs nothing to be gentlemanly, does it?

DENISE	I suppose not. I just wish more men would try it. I think it would get them further than they think. Further than throwing their weight around anyway. Women like to be nurtured, no matter how many shelves they can put up, or tyres they can change.
TONY	*(having taken her coat carefully, now just tosses it over the back of a chair and pulls out another chair, on which she sits).* There's nothing wrong with a woman who can change a tyre or put up a shelf. I've never found it an unattractive quality. In fact, quite the opposite. *(Sitting)*
DENISE	Well, of course, I'm no stranger to a toolbox.
TONY	You don't say.
DENISE	I'm quite the face in Screwfix.
TONY	Really.
DENISE	Oh yes. They always have a little laugh with me. "Hard at it again this weekend, are we?" They find that most amusing.
TONY	I'll bet. Just waiting for you to come in and ask for a new ball cock.
DENISE	What? Oh; you're pulling my leg, aren't you?
TONY	Would I?
DENISE	Well; I don't know, do I? I don't really know you. I mean; we've barely spoken at work, so it was quite a surprise that you asked me. *(Looking around, dubiously).* What is this place?
TONY	I like it. It's… reasonably priced. I thought you might like it too.
DENISE	*(unconvinced)* It's… dated, isn't it? But I do like it. Really.

TONY	Good. *(Indicates teapot and cups on the tables)* Anyway, I took the liberty of ordering tea. Proper leaves. I know you drink it that way.
DENISE	Oh. How thoughtful! How did you know that?
TONY	Sandra's seen you making it in the kitchen at work. With that little china man that you put the leaves in and hang over the edge of the mug.
DENISE	Kenneth.
TONY	Kenneth?
DENISE	Yes. That's his name. It seems rude not to give him a name when he's scalding his unmentionables morning and night for my pleasure.
TONY	Well; quite. Sandra says he looks like he's in a hot tub. Hanging his arms over the back of the mug. I'm glad I ordered the tea, since you haven't had a proper one today.
DENISE	It was very thoughtful. *(Pause)* You asked your secretary how I take my tea?
TONY	Well. Yes. Women are so much better at that sort of thing. Thinking of the right thing to do. I wanted everything to be right.
DENISE	You did?
TONY	Of course. *(He breaks the slightly awkward silence by handing her the menu)* So: what will it be?
DENISE	I don't know. I don't get asked out for breakfast. What should I have?
TONY	Anything you like. Eggs Florentine. Mashed avocado on toast....
DENISE	They'd do that here? What's eggs Florentine?
TONY	Most places will do whatever you ask for. You just need to ask in the right way. It's all about confidence.

DENISE	*(looking down at the menu)* I think you might need insane amounts of confidence to get eggs Florentine, whatever they are, out of this place. And as for avocado… you might get banana.
TONY	*(taking the menu from her)* Ok. Forget that. If you could have anything at all, what would that be? But you have to give me your reasons.
DENISE	Anything?
TONY	*(leaning forwards)* Absolutely anything. But I have to know the reason why.
DENISE	You do?
TONY	Yes. Isn't that why we're here. To get to know each other better?
DENISE	Well, I suppose it must be.
TONY	So: tell me.
DENISE	What I'd most like to eat? Out of everything?
TONY	Well; for breakfast. We have to start somewhere.
DENISE	Yes. I suppose we do. *(She thinks for a few seconds)* Ok. What I'd like more than anything is an almond croissant. A fresh one. There!
TONY	Ok. Go on.
DENISE	What?
TONY	Why do you want that?
DENISE	*(closing her eyes, smiling, as she speaks)* Because a man bought me one in Paris. Warm and crumbly. *(Opening her eyes and looking at him meaningfully)* Then he kissed the crumbs from my lips.
TONY	*(suddenly wrong-footed)* Right. I'll see what I can do.

DENISE	Oh, don't panic. Look; let's forget about food for now and be honest with each other, shall we?
TONY	How do you mean?
DENISE	Why did you really ask me to meet you this morning?
TONY	You seem nice. I like you. I wanted to get to know you. Why else?
DENISE	Well, thank you. I am nice. And it would be nice to believe that. But, actually, now I'm here, I don't.
TONY	But it's true.
DENISE	Please. I'm not naïve, and I don't wish to be patronised. You have a nice suit, and a nice car. A typical, successful man. I'm not exactly your type, am I?
TONY	Don't you think that's just as patronising? You have no idea what 'my type' is. Or if I have one. Do you? *(Giving up, leans back exhaling)* All right. I'm sorry. I misread you, clearly. The truth is: I need your help.
DENISE	My help? For what? And what makes you think I'll be inclined to help you?
TONY	I'm taking a big risk, I know. But Sandra says you're trustworthy. I asked her to tell you things in confidence. To ask you not to spread them round. Oh; things that really it wouldn't matter if you did because most of them aren't true but…
DENISE	…and I'd look like an idiot if I did?
TONY	Don't be like that. At least hear me out. And if you say no, and give the game away, then to be honest my life can't get any worse.
DENISE	*(standing)* Thank you for the tea. I'll see you at work. And no; I won't tell anyone about this very strange encounter. Which I'm failing to understand.
TONY	Wait. Look: I know you're not like all the others. I can see that. You're different. Not a drone. I've seen you

sitting at your desk, staring into space. You keep a pen in your hair.

DENISE   You've noticed a lot.

TONY   I've made it my business to. Please. Just listen. You can walk out if you want.

DENISE   *(sitting)* Ok. But this had better be good.

TONY   I don't really know where to start. I wasn't expecting to do this now.

DENISE   Start at the beginning.

TONY   Alright. Six months ago, my wife left me. She took everything. And I mean everything. Not just the children and the contents of the bank account, but the bed linen, the lightbulbs from the ceiling, the cat flap. The cat flap for God's sake. Left me with a massive hole in the back door. She left the cat, incidentally. Because she knows it hates me, the furry bastard.

DENISE   *(laughing)* What did you do? What was it? Drink? Other women? You must have really pissed her off. What is it you've got a weakness for Tony?

TONY   Oh I've got lots of weaknesses. And yes; she had lots of very good reasons. So; I have a nice suit, which I can keep, and a nice car, which I can't. And a massive amount of debt. My house is remortgaged so many times over it's not even worth trying to sell it. I might as well just leave the keys on the table and walk away. Most of my debts are to some very unpleasant people. And I mean seriously unpleasant. If I can't sort this out, I'm looking at ending up in the Thames. And not on a pleasure cruise.

DENISE   I see. Well; you have got yourself in a bit of a pickle, haven't you?

TONY   You could say that.

DENISE   So, I assume this has got something to do with me being in the payroll department?

7

TONY   You win five pounds. Or you would if I had it.

DENISE   And, what? And there I was. The oddball in the payroll department. A single lady who goes home to her cat every night. Mine doesn't hate me, by the way. So, what did you and Sandra think? I'd be easy to charm? Throw her a bone. She doesn't get much attention. Get me under your spell and I'd do anything you ask? Make off with the payroll, and before you know it, I'm in the cells and you and Sandra are in Lanzarote.

TONY   Look, it wasn't like that.

DENISE   Oh no? The problem for you is that women stick together. Sandra doesn't trust you, Tony. Not as far as she can throw you. She's one of your weaknesses, isn't she? And one of the reasons your wife left you. But she's far from stupid. She knows full well that if you can do that to one woman, you'll do it to another. So, she took out insurance. With me.

TONY   What do you mean?

DENISE   Well, all those times she was supposedly feeding me your lies to spread around, she was telling me all about you, and her. And this plan. How she was sure you'd leave her to take the blame, along with me. But I took out insurance too. I recorded the conversations.

TONY   You scheming….

DENISE   Now, now. Let's keep it civil.

TONY   So you knew all along? Even before I asked you to meet me?

DENISE   Of course. I was very intrigued as to how you'd go about it. I thought I'd string you along a bit. See how far you'd go. But I couldn't do it. Like I said: I'm nice.

TONY   Conversations like that mean nothing. What do you think you can do with those?

DENISE   I'm not sure yet. I'm sure they'd get you the sack, and you really need this job. But luckily for you; just as

8

	Sandra doesn't trust you, and I don't trust you, neither do I entirely trust her. And I certainly don't like her. So I'm inclined to help you, because I can. But entirely on my own terms, and when I say.
TONY	Jesus. I might as well call myself Kenneth.
DENISE	What: balls-deep in hot water for my entertainment? I suppose so, yes. I think I might just keep you there. But at least I can keep you alive.
TONY	So what happens now?
DENISE	Well, I'm not keen on this place, and I've worked up quite a hunger. So, I think you should take me somewhere far nicer. And you can pay.
TONY	Yes; I imagine I will be.

Lights down. They exit, carrying the teapot and cups, Tony SL, Denise SR. They change into different daytime business clothes. While the lights are still down, they re-enter and sit, with a wine glass and a coffee cup.

Scene 2

Lights up. A man and a woman are seated at a table, on opposite sides to the previous couple. She has wine. He has coffee.

GRACE Well. It's been a while. I was surprised to hear from you.

ADRIAN You know how it is. Time goes by. I'm busy. Karen; the kids….

GRACE Those poor bloody children. You've blamed them for your having no time for the past 17 years. And Karen never sees you!

ADRIAN Karen never sees me because I'm out at work keeping her in new cars and furniture and all those things she loves so much. You know that full well, as does she. She can't have it both ways.

GRACE So you keep saying.

ADRIAN *(looking round)* Anyway, what is this place?

GRACE I like it. It's… basic. Shabby chic, I suppose.

ADRIAN And you do love all that pretentious crap. Your house is filled with it. Shabby chic might be pushing it a bit. This place hasn't been touched in decades.

GRACE I like it. And at least I don't live in a white box. Scared to breathe in case I mess the place up.

ADRIAN That's how Karen likes it. And I've got used to it.

GRACE It makes me nervous.

ADRIAN Does it? And when do you ever come and see us to know that? The kids would love to see you sometimes, you know. And Karen. You know how fond of you they are. God knows why. Anyway; it's honest at least. I don't try to make out that an Aga isn't out of place in a three year-old house.

GRACE I don't know why it annoys you so much.

ADRIAN	Well, it does. It's… fraudulent.
GRACE	I have nobody but myself to please. The children never come near the place unless they want something, and it'll be a cold day in hell before I shack up with anyone again. I like it on my own.
ADRIAN	Oh, don't do the burning martyr act.
GRACE	I'm not. I do. It's far better than being in the shackles of somebody else's expectations.
ADRIAN	It doesn't have to be like that.
GRACE	Oh no? And what about you?
ADRIAN	It isn't like that for me, you know that. I'm just better at compromise than you've ever been.
GRACE	Compromise? Under the thumb more like. When do you ever get to do anything for yourself? Working yourself to a standstill for the sake of other people.
ADRIAN	Other people who I love. I'm happy, Grace. Unlike you. I've watched you for so many years refusing to be happy, when everyone around you has tried to make you so.
GRACE	God; why are we doing this? And why are we arguing about my taste in decorating?
ADRIAN	We've got to argue about something.
GRACE	I suppose we do.
ADRIAN	You know, I always thought we'd grow out of it. Be like normal people; raise our children together in one big happy family. Never really worked out like that, has it?
GRACE	No. I suppose not. But the children all get on. And they're old enough to make up their own minds.

11

ADRIAN	I just don't know why you've never been able to put it all behind you, like I have. It wasn't that bad, and you know it. You've always had to twist things.
GRACE	God. I need another drink. You see, this is what happens. Every time. *(She raises her glass over her shoulder, towards the bar, for a refill)*
ADRIAN	Grace; don't….
GRACE	Oh piss off! I'm not Dad. And I'm not about to fall off the wagon again. *(Studies him for a few seconds)* You look at me exactly how you used to look at him.
ADRIAN	For God's sake. I'm not looking at you in any way. I didn't come here to argue with you. *(Looking around)* This place is so dark….
GRACE	Adrian; I have to be back at work in half an hour. What do you want?
ADRIAN	I wanted to see you because I need to talk to you about Mum.
GRACE	*(putting her glass down)* Right.
ADRIAN	Look, I know it upsets you.
GRACE	It doesn't. I just try not to think about it.
ADRIAN	I don't understand this. I never have. How you can just switch off.
GRACE	She is being well looked after. We don't have to worry. She's far better where she is, and we both know that.
ADRIAN	When did you last go to see her?
GRACE	She doesn't know who we are. There seems very little point.
ADRIAN	That's not true. The staff always say it's not. And even if it is, it makes her better when we've been. When we've all been. The children all go. Karen goes when she can. Mike goes….

GRACE	Oh don't bring him into it.
ADRIAN	He doesn't have to, Grace. But he does because he cares about her. Even Jodie visits.
GRACE	Well; the woman's a saint. We all know that.
ADRIAN	Right. Whatever. I'm not here to listen to your bitterness. I want to talk about what's best for Mum.
GRACE	I've already given my opinion. She is best where she is. I don't see any need to change that.
ADRIAN	I've been talking to the staff. Well, Karen and I have. They think that she could be at home, with live-in care. Back in familiar surroundings. It might just help. Some memories are starting to come back. She can walk quite well. The talking will come....
GRACE	What? Are you both completely mad?
ADRIAN	We have to decide what to do with the house anyway. If she's never going back to it, we can't keep hold of it.
GRACE	I've told you before that I've got no interest in the house. Sell it, for all I care. It can be for Karen and the kids. Mum would want you to have it anyway.
ADRIAN	That's the problem, though. We sell it and Mum gets even better. Then she has to come home. You know we can't have her at our place...
GRACE	Oh no. Don't even think about suggesting that she comes to live with me.
ADRIAN	I'm not suggesting it. Not yet. She'd have a live-in carer in her own home. We could be there whenever we can. There are enough of us to do it. And we should all want to, Grace. She's our mother. I know it's difficult now, but we've been lucky.
GRACE	Have we now?
ADRIAN	You know we have. An accident like that could have been the end of her.

GRACE	Maybe it should've.
ADRIAN	Christ! I've been really patient with you, Grace. For years. Everyone has. Mike was patient. He saw how Dad was, and how you were, He understood that. But that's all in the past now. We couldn't save Dad, and I thought you were in recovery. And Mum protected us from all that.
GRACE	And Dad always gets the blame.
ADRIAN	And why shouldn't he? It was awful; what his drinking did to us all. To Mum especially. But he was ill, Grace. You of all people should understand that.
GRACE	*(starting to laugh)* God, Adrian. He wasn't ill at all. He was driven to it. By her.
ADRIAN	What the hell are you talking about?
GRACE	You accuse me of having no feelings. It's the absolute opposite.
ADRIAN	You need to start making some sort of sense.
GRACE	She never protected you from anything. It was me. I never wanted to tell you, but you need to know why I can't be near her. Ever.
ADRIAN	What are you trying to say?
GRACE	It was her, Adrian. Not him. She's evil. I knew it from when I was tiny. Right from when they adopted you.
ADRIAN	*(stands)* Not this again. This is boring Grace. I've heard it for years. Years of teenage ranting and drunken phone calls. I was the favourite, the one they chose after the disappointing girl had come along. I know that's what you think. The excuse you've always used for your life being a mess, when in reality it's just you that's set to self-destruct. Change the record.
GRACE	It's not just what I think. It's what I know. And I know because she told me. For years. Just me. Whispering in my ears. Notes in my school bag. All about how useless

14

I was, and how she'd waited for you to come along. In front of you it was different. She couldn't hold it all in – it was clear you were her favourite. I couldn't hide that. But it went so far beyond that. So far that I thought everyone would think I was mad if I said anything. She told me they would. Dad was no use, because she did the same to him.

ADRIAN   I don't believe this. Why tell me now? Why haven't you said anything for all these years? I can understand a child, a teenager, being afraid of not being believed. But a grown woman? It's pathetic. You're just finding excuses for your own weaknesses. And as for Dad being driven to it? This isn't a play. It's real life. He was an alcoholic, Grace. Plain and simple. And so are you.

GRACE   Why didn't I tell you? You've just answered your own question.

ADRIAN   You're ill too, Grace. But we can get you some help. *(Moves to sit in the third chair, next to Grace)*

GRACE   I don't want your help. I just want you to understand what I'm trying to tell you. It's alright for you. You don't have their blood in your veins. But I do. His 'weakness'; her monstrousness. Maybe that's why she hated me so much. She could see that I was just another version of her. And him. She hated them both. You; well, you were different. You could be anything she wanted you to be.

ADRIAN   I think you should stop now. Forget work. I'll take you home.

GRACE   It didn't stop when I left home, you know. And I went as early as I could. Do you remember? To that flat above the chemist. Sixteen and scared and broke, and she let everyone think I was practically a prostitute. Such a disappointment. She'd send me notes, telling me to kill myself and have done with it. She'd poison any relationship I ever had. Call my boss at work pretending to be past employers. She drove my husband away. And my children....

ADRIAN   Grace….

GRACE   What kind of woman does that? To her own daughter?

ADRIAN   But you saved her life. The doctors said if you hadn't acted so quickly after the accident, she'd be dead.

GRACE   *(begins to laugh again)*

ADRIAN   Nothing about this is funny.

GRACE   But don't you see? I pushed her.

ADRIAN   What?

GRACE   I pushed her. Or I let her fall. Either way I didn't stop her from falling. She'd followed me upstairs. Nag, nag, nagging in her usual way. I turned around, and there she was. Losing her grip on the banister. It was so easy. She held her hand out to me, but I just stepped back. And there she went: the whole way down. But I couldn't follow it through. Couldn't leave her. My dear mother who'd called around when I was out, taken a tumble and been found too late. Weak; you see. Like she always said I was. She'd despise me for it.

ADRIAN   I've no idea where to even begin with this.

GRACE   You can do whatever you want. You know now. I don't care if you hate me. I lost everything a long time ago.

ADRIAN   Grace, I don't hate you. I….

GRACE   Please don't tell me you feel sorry for me.

ADRIAN   I don't. I'm trying to understand you. Let's go. I'll take you home and you can tell me everything. From the beginning.

GRACE   I don't think so.

ADRIAN   We can start again. From today. Try to put some of this right.

GRACE   I don't think that will work. How can it?

16

ADRIAN   I've no idea. But we can try. And we can start by getting out of this place.

GRACE   *(smiling slightly)* I suppose we can.

Lights down and they exit SL. Lights must be completely down before they move, as they are not exiting to the door. They change into costumes for John and Linda.

Interlude

Lights up as John and Linda enter SL. Linda carries a cocktail, John a candle and lighter. Linda puts the cocktail down by the seat on SR. John tries and fails to light the lighter, then just tips the candle upside down, which lights it.

LINDA   *(looking at the table)* You've forgotten the water jug.

John takes the flowers out of the vase, and points to it. Linda gives him a look. The refrain from 'Oranges and Lemons' sounds. They look upwards, at each other and then out to the audience. John exits SL, Linda SR. Lights down. They change into clothes suitable for the end of a night out.

Scene 3

Lights up. It is very late (or very early). A woman sits at a table with a ridiculous green cocktail filled with fruit and umbrellas in front of her. A man joins her from the direction of the bar, holding a whiskey tumbler. They are smartly dressed, but slightly dishevelled at the end of a long night out. There is an air of argumentative good humour between them.

SIMON	What is this place anyway?
ANGIE	I like it. And it was near. When did you get so particular?
SIMON	I'm not. What the hell are you drinking?
ANGIE	No idea. It looked good on the cocktail menu. I thought fruit might sober me up. Or something. But seeing you always does that anyway.
SIMON	Thanks. You didn't have to agree to meet me you know.
ANGIE	I know. But I was having a rotten night and thought I could do with a laugh.
SIMON	At my expense?
ANGIE	Always. You walk into it, you know that.
SIMON	*(looking around again)* What the hell is this place?
ANGIE	Repeating yourself isn't going to make it any better.
SIMON	It's weird. And there's nothing later than the early 60s on the jukebox. And I doubt that's intentional. Why couldn't we meet somewhere we know?
ANGIE	Neutral ground is best. You know that. Especially when I don't know what you want. And when I think I'm not going to like what you want. I don't want to tip this bloody ridiculous drink all over you. It cost an arm and a leg. But a place with memories would probably make it unavoidable. So; what's she done now?

SIMON	Why do you think she's done anything? Maybe I just wanted to see you.
ANGIE	*(laughing)* You never 'just want to see me'. You never have. There's always something. I don't know why you bother. I'll just stick a plaster on it and send you back home. I can't make things better; I haven't been able to for years. *(She picks up her drink, tries to work her way around the umbrellas. Fails)* Christ!
SIMON	What's in that. Absinthe?
ANGIE	Probably. God knows. And melon, for some reason. And what looks suspiciously like Jelly Tots. It's like something Picasso puked up!
SIMON	You always have liked stupid drinks. Children's drinks.
ANGIE	I know. You tell me practically every time we meet.
SIMON	And children's food. Burger places and horrible fried chicken.
ANGIE	Oh, sod off.
SIMON	I never have been able to make you appreciate the finer things in life.
ANGIE	I suppose you think that includes why I never wanted to marry you?
SIMON	I gave up on that years ago. You've never wanted to marry anyone.
ANGIE	I'm not wasting expensive underwear on a husband.
SIMON	So who are you wasting it on? You might as well waste it on someone who might stick around for more than ten minutes. Someone that you might just feel something for.
ANGIE	God. You know my feelings on that. Mad passion is fine. But sooner or later you're having a blazing row about something stupid in Tesco, and that's that. Forever. *(Miming quote marks)* Till death do you part.

SIMON	*(ruefully)* Not necessarily.
ANGIE	That's my point. I'm not like you. I'd stick at it, rather than run as soon as someone else takes my fancy. Even if it made me bloody miserable! Because I'm stubborn and idiotic. That's why I can't take the risk. I've never found any man on the face of the planet, well almost never, who has been worth the risk. You know how many times I've tried. And I've seen your track record. *(Laughing)* You don't *have* to keep marrying them for Christ's sake.
SIMON	*(laughing)* Trouble is, I do. You know me. It's all or nothing. So: why the rotten night? You look lovely, by the way.
ANGIE	Thank you. I don't. I look how I feel. *(Pause)* Do you really want to know?
SIMON	No. Yes… I worry about you.
ANGIE	And you'd worry less if I had a husband?
SIMON	I'd worry less if I thought you weren't out night after night, taking home God knows who.
ANGIE	They are always terribly respectable. You know that's the kind of man I meet. I have a massive salary. I go to expensive places.
SIMON	*(looking round)* So I see.
ANGIE	My shoes cost more than your last wedding!
SIMON	*(laughing)* So why the bad night?
ANGIE	It wasn't actually. It was going very well. I was having a wonderful time with a very beautiful man, who was promising that the whole night was about to get a whole lot better.
SIMON	Then why come here?
ANGIE	Because they are very easy to find. This city is full of men like that. Beautiful men in expensive suits, buying

	expensive drinks, who want a woman in expensive shoes and expensive underwear to tell them how brilliant they are. Men are so easy to work. You just massage their egos.
SIMON	Don't be so cynical.
ANGIE	Why not? It's true. You're no different. God, my bra's digging in. I thought I'd be taking it off by now.
SIMON	For God's sake….
ANGIE	And I need a cigarette. *(Indicating the door)* Do you mind…?
SIMON	*(increasingly angry)* Yes. I do mind. I asked you to meet me and you agreed to. You could have said no, and you didn't. At least do me the courtesy of not making out I bore you to tears and you can't wait to head for the door. It's childish. You are childish. And fucking selfish.
ANGIE	I've never pretended to be anything else.
SIMON	And that isn't true. You were never like this, and you know that as well as I do.
ANGIE	Maybe I was and you just never knew me.
SIMON	That's bollocks and you know it.
ANGIE	Why do we keep doing this? Every time. It's just a pointless circular conversation that gets us nowhere.
SIMON	Because this is our life now. Forever. And there is no getting away from that. All we have is each other; whether we like that or not. All these years of not knowing. While we don't know.
ANGIE	*(standing)* That's it. I'm going. I can't keep doing this month after month, year after year. Go home. Be happy. Buy a dog.
SIMON	*(Stopping her from leaving)* I've heard something. About him. I've heard something.

ANGIE	*(Sitting)* Oh God. Please don't do this.
SIMON	That's why I wanted to see you. I've heard something.
ANGIE	You always do. We always do. And it's never anything. He doesn't want us to find him. He hates us that much.
SIMON	He doesn't hate us. We're his parents.
ANGIE	He does. He must. To do that. To do *this.*
SIMON	He can't. He was happy. I know we weren't a traditional family, but we never fought. We were always kind to each other.
ANGIE	Was he? We were so young. He could see he'd tied us together when we never should have been. That he stopped us doing all those things we should have done.
SIMON	But we never minded that. Not really.
ANGIE	Didn't we? He could see it. He could. He must have; and felt so broken by it. He wanted to punish us in the worst way possible. The worst. Our own son, and we couldn't see it.
SIMON	These people… they think they've found a lead. In Singapore.
ANGIE	God; it was Australia last time. Please; don't do this.
SIMON	They seem reliable. These people. You ring them if you've lost someone and they tell you who to contact. The police think it's a reliable source, in Singapore. I'm going to go out there, and I want you to come with me. He needs to see both of us.
ANGIE	No. Another dead end. I can't bear it. *(Stands)*
SIMON	Please. Sit down. I'll get us some coffee…

Lights down as he collects their glasses and she sits. Lights down. They exit SL to change back into John and Linda.

Scene 4

Lights up. It is the end of the night. The bar staff have just cleared out the last of the customers. John enters SL, pauses to dump the flowers back in the vase, and goes over to the door, which is being banged on.

JOHN *(speaking off)* No…. Right… for God's sake; I've tried to help. Just get him off the front step. Is he…? Oh Jesus. I'm shutting the door.

LINDA *(enters from SL carrying a tea cup with 'Kenneth' sitting in it)* Don't tell me…

JOHN *(reappears from SR, carrying an absinthe bottle, which he puts on the table)* Yes. All over the step. And he's collapsed face-down in it. We can't leave him like that. Not all night.

LINDA No. He'll sober up and stagger off at some point. And if he doesn't…. well, it could be worse.

JOHN Oh, I know. We've seen it all over the years though, haven't we?

LINDA Tell me about it. Far worse.

JOHN Yes, but we deal with it and move on.

LINDA Haven't got a lot of choice.

JOHN No.

There is sound of banging at the door.

LINDA We have to get rid of them. Go and have a word.

JOHN Ok.

Goes to the side of the stage and speaks off. Linda picks up the absinthe bottle, unscrew the cap, sniffs it, pours some into her cup and drinks. John returns.

They want to come in and call for a taxi.

LINDA	*(a noise sounds from above. She glances upwards)* Well, they can't. We can't have them back in now. There's no reason for them to come back in. No reason at all.
JOHN	They'll just keep banging on the door.
LINDA	We can put up with that. For now, anyway. It happens now and again. They just can't see that when we're closed, we really are closed.
JOHN	*(looking around)* Well, it's a bit of a mess in here, so we'd better get on.
LINDA	We have to find someone to take over. We can't just keep doing this forever.
JOHN	We will find them eventually. The right people just never seem to come along.
LINDA	Which is odd, as only the 'right people' ever find their way in here. They're the only people who *can* find it.
JOHN	Sadly, though, never to do the bottling-up, or to clean the gents'. That bloody ball cock.
LINDA	It's a good job nobody ever gets around to ordering food. The drinks we can cope with.
JOHN	Close though. We just about manage to stop them.
LINDA	We do. It's hard sometimes. They don't always do quite what you want them to.
JOHN	But, we have to keep trying. If we ever want to get out of here.
LINDA	Whatever we do doesn't ever seem to be quite enough.

The banging continues on the door.

JOHN	Look; why don't we let them in? I know it's not worked before, but how long is it since we've tried it?

LINDA	Because it won't work. You can't think that way. We've tried it, and it didn't. They're not the right ones. We obviously can't repeat. It needs to be different.
JOHN	How long is it since that was us? Knocking on the door to use the phone.
LINDA	God; when was it? 1963. After the works' Christmas party. *(She starts to smile, then stops)* I try not to think about it. Where they thought we'd gone. How long they must've searched.
JOHN	You can't help it. I wonder if they still do. After all these years.
LINDA	I just think about how happy they were. The previous two. She took my face in her hands *(she demonstrates on him)* and said 'I've found you'.
JOHN	And they were gone. *('Oranges and Lemons' sounds from above. They both look up)*
LINDA	We can't say they weren't prepared.
JOHN	Who knows how long they'd been waiting for us. They didn't seem to want to stay and chat.
LINDA	It could have been any length of time. They must have been desperate.
JOHN	We know how that feels.
LINDA	We can't rush it, though. I sometimes wonder if it's just coincidence that we arrived together, and they got away together. Whether one of us will leave and the other won't....
JOHN	No. Both of us leave or we both stay. I don't think I could face whatever is outside of this place on my own. Not what I've got to go back to.
LINDA	How will we face it anyway? How do we explain where we've been?

JOHN	We can't worry about that. We have to think about getting out of here.
LINDA	So: what do we think?
JOHN	Of today's lot? Well, we've managed to get some of them back in. One of the men and two of the women. A little bit better this time, but clearly still not good enough.
LINDA	Because we're still here and they're still out there? Living their various chaotic lives.
JOHN	Living them, though.
LINDA	Do we try them again?
JOHN	Why not? A little rewrite of each. I'm still not happy about the mother.
LINDA	I agree. *(Takes a notepad from her apron, and a pen from her hair).* I still think it should be dementia, not an accident.
JOHN	You might be right. What about the others?
LINDA	I'm wondering whether we're getting the pairings wrong. Whether we should mix them up a bit?
JOHN	I'm willing to try anything.

A noise sounds from above. They both look up, then look at each other.

LINDA	We'd better get started….

Lights fade to blackout.

The End

Lost and Found

A Dark Comedy
by
Ashley Burgoyne

Cast

Lucy (*40s, the only worker in a support-line call centre*)
Philip (*40s, her new colleague*)

Scene One

Day One. Two desks, or tables, downstage centre. Each table has a laptop, or some other PC, with quite a low screen so Lucy and Philip can be seen easily over the top. One desk is pretty sparse. The other desk is much busier. Small potted plant, odd photo and a 'desk tidy' with pencils etc.

Behind the busy desk sits Lucy, 40's. She has a telephonist headset on, but isn't currently talking to anyone. She is filing her nails. After a moment she picks up her large handbag, from next to her chair, and ferrets around in it for a bit and eventually pulls out a packet of Hula Hoops. She opens the packet and crunches through a couple very noisily. She then starts to place them on her fingers.

LUCY *(looking down at her fingers)* When did you all get so fat? *(Pause)* I used to be able to push you all the way down to make proper rings. *(Pause)* I got married to my neighbour, Freddie, when I was five with one of these. *(In a vicar's voice!)* I now pronounce you Lucy and Freddie. You may kiss in the Wendy House! *(She chuckles to herself. Looking at her fingers, again)* Oh, well. At least they're easier to get off this way! *(She pulls the Hula Hoops off the ends of her fingers, one at a time, with her teeth)*

The phone rings.

(With a start) Bloody hell! A phone call! *(She presses a button on the keyboard and starts speaking into her headset)* Hello; Lost and Found. My name's Lucy, how can I be of assistance…? Yes… right… I see… well, no, it's not exactly what I'm here for, but I'm sure I can find the number for you. Which train was it?

At this point Philip, 40's, enters. He is dressed quite smartly but is nervous. He is approaching very cautiously. When he sees Lucy engaged in conversation, he stops short of the desks.

Yarmouth… right… here we go…try this 03456007245. They should be a little more help than me. *(She notices Philip and gives a little wave. Philip*

	returns the wave) You're welcome… take care… bye, bye. *(She presses another key on the keyboard)* Blimey! *(removing her headset and rising, offering her hand to Philip)* Hello. You must be Philip?
PHILIP	*(Shaking hands)* Yes, that's right, hello.
LUCY	Hello.
PHILIP	Hello. *(The handshake ends and there's an awkward silence)* I'm sorry, but I'm afraid you have me at a disadvantage.
LUCY	Sorry?
PHILIP	You know my name, but I don't know yours.
LUCY	What!? Oh, yes. Sorry. I'm Lucy.
PHILIP	Lucy? Oh, lovely…
LUCY	*(interjecting)* Oh, thank you.
PHILIP	…name.
LUCY	Sorry?
PHILIP	Your name; Lucy. It's a lovely name.
LUCY	*(slightly embarrassed)* Oh, my name. Yes. Thank you.
PHILIP	You're welcome.
LUCY	Sorry. Because I had a memo with your name on, I assumed you'd had one with my name on!
PHILIP	Oh, right, I see. No. All I had was an address.
LUCY	Ah, right. Find us alright, did you?
PHILIP	Well, not exactly.

LUCY	Ah.
PHILIP	I could see my destination. The satnav kept telling me I was at my destination. But the one-way system seemed to keep taking me away from my destination.
LUCY	Yes, well, I'm afraid it is a bit like that out there.
PHILIP	Quite extraordinary.
LUCY	Yes.
PHILIP	Whatever lane I tried, I seemed to be in the wrong one when I came around again.
LUCY	That sounds just about right.
PHILIP	Extraordinary.
LUCY	Indeed.
PHILIP	Then, on the fourth or fifth time round I met a tractor coming the other way.
LUCY	*(looking at her watch)* Ah, yes, you would at around this time.
PHILIP	Really!?
LUCY	Yes. Blue tractor?
PHILIP	Yes.
LUCY	Yes. That'll be Barry.
PHILIP	Barry?
LUCY	Local farmer. On the town council. He was the only one to vote against the new one-way system four years ago. So; refuses to use it.
PHILIP	Extraordinary! How does he get away with it?

35

LUCY	He's a landowner and, as I said, he's on the town council.
PHILIP	Oh. Right. I see.

Pause

LUCY	*(offering a seat)* Anyway, you're here now. Here's your desk!
PHILIP	*(taking the seat)* My desk?
LUCY	*(sitting at her desk)* Yes. Unless you'd rather have mine? I can easily move all my bits across.
PHILIP	No, no. This desk is fine. It's just that where I came from you get a different desk whenever you come in for a shift.
LUCY	*(quite taken aback)* Really?
PHILIP	Oh yes. Come in. Find a desk. Pop on headset and away you go!
LUCY	*(looking at all her paraphernalia on her desk)* So, no one has pictures and plants and things on their desk.
PHILIP	No.
LUCY	That seems quite sad to me.
PHILIP	Well, yes, I suppose it is really. But it was very busy there.
LUCY	Where were you?
PHILIP	Oh, er, Watford.
LUCY	Oh, right. I've never been there.
PHILIP	No?

LUCY	No. *(Pause)* Should I bother?
PHILIP	What with?
LUCY	Going to Watford.
PHILIP	Oh, erm, no. I shouldn't.
LUCY	Right.
PHILIP	I've been trying to get out of there for quite a while myself!
LUCY	Oh, right.
PHILIP	Yes.

Pause

PHILIP	So, if this is my desk and that's yours. Where does everyone else sit?
LUCY	Everyone else?
PHILIP	Yes. You know; other shifts, and so on.
LUCY	*(laughing)* Didn't they tell you?
PHILIP	Tell me what?
LUCY	That I'm the only person here!
PHILIP	What? That's not possible! I mean, who mans the phones when you're not here?
LUCY	No one.
PHILIP	No one? But what if someone's lost when no one's here? Does it get transferred to another branch?
LUCY	*(laughing)* No! It goes to answerphone.

PHILIP	*(in disbelief)* Answerphone!?
LUCY	Yes; and I go through the messages in the morning.
PHILIP	This all sounds very slipshod compared to Watford.
LUCY	*(slightly disgruntled)* Well; I'm sorry if I'm not up to the standards you're used to in Watford.
PHILIP	No, no. I'm sorry Lucy. I didn't mean to offend you. It's not you I'm having a go at.
LUCY	Well, it sounds like it.
PHILIP	No, no. Definitely not you. It's Lost and Found I'm having a go at. They don't seem to have sorted you out properly here.
LUCY	I think I need to explain a few things to you, Philip.
PHILIP	Erm, yes. You quite possibly do.
LUCY	This branch of Lost and Found has only been open about four months. Did you know that?
PHILIP	Well, I knew it was quite new.
LUCY	First one in Norfolk.
PHILIP	Right.
LUCY	Go on, then.
PHILIP	Sorry?
LUCY	Ask me what everyone asks at this point.
PHILIP	*(a little stuck)* Erm, right…. No, I'm sorry; what does everyone ask you at this point?
LUCY	Why, if we're the first branch in Norfolk, aren't we in Norwich?

PHILIP	Oh, right.
LUCY	Go on, then.
PHILIP	Sorry?
LUCY	Ask me.
PHILIP	Oh, right, I see. You actually want me to ask you?
LUCY	*(nodding)* Uh-huh.
PHILIP	Right. Erm… Lucy, if this is the first branch of Lost and Found in Norfolk, why isn't it in Norwich?
LUCY	Funny you should ask that, Philip. Overheads.
PHILIP	Sorry?
LUCY	Overheads.
PHILIP	Oh, right, I see. And that's it?
LUCY	Isn't that enough?
PHILIP	Well, I suppose it is. I just thought that with all the build up there might have been other reasons.
LUCY	As a charity, Philip, overheads is the only reason we need.
PHILIP	Yes. Indeed. I'm still not sure why Watford has fifteen desks, with at least ten being manned 24/7 and the whole of Norfolk has you!
LUCY	There are two reasons for this, Philip.
PHILIP	*(thinking)* Ah, yes, well I think I've got one of them.
LUCY	Go on.

PHILIP	Is one reason Watford? I mean, I know you haven't been there, but it's worlds away from Norfolk.
LUCY	That is one reason, Philip. And the other is that no one has found Lost and Found yet.
PHILIP	Oh, right. I see. I think.
LUCY	Round here people keep their problems to themselves. They're not the sharing type. A pint down the pub, a stroll on the beach and they think they're right as rain.
PHILIP	I see. And are they?
LUCY	Are they what?
PHILIP	Right as rain?
LUCY	How would I know. No one ever phones!
PHILIP	Ah.
LUCY	And let's just say if the pint doesn't work then there's always the short pier at Cromer where the occasional person can take a long walk. If you know what I mean?
PHILIP	I think I follow you.
LUCY	Good. As long as you don't follow them!
PHILIP	Quite!
LUCY	Although they sometimes struggle.
PHILIP	Who do?
LUCY	The people trying to end it all at the end of the pier.
PHILIP	Why's that?
LUCY	Well, there's a lifeboat ramp into the sea at the end of the pier.

40

PHILIP	Right.
LUCY	So not as dramatic as hurling yourself off a great height.
PHILIP	No. Quite literally a long walk off a short pier!
LUCY	Exactly! One person tried to finish himself off by walking down the ramp into the sea when the lifeboat house was open to the public.
PHILIP	Right.
LUCY	The coxswain saw him heading towards the waves and launched the lifeboat so bloody quickly there was more chance of him being run over by the lifeboat than there was of being drowned!
PHILIP	My word!
LUCY	*(chuckling)* And, of course, they're all rather stuck in their ways around here.
PHILIP	What do you mean?
LUCY	I'm sure that if they're in need of any help they'll phone an established helpline such as The Samaritans or Childline; you know?
PHILIP	Yes. Although you were on the phone when I came in. So, some people must be finding the number.
LUCY	Ah; yes. But, did you actually listen to my end of the conversation?
PHILIP	Well, no. Not really. I'd only just walked in and I didn't want to appear rude.
LUCY	Well, if you had, you'd have heard me giving her the phone number for lost property at Great Yarmouth Train Station!

PHILIP   Really!? Why?

LUCY   Because she'd left her brolly on the 8:05 to Yarmouth and she thought Lost and Found could find it!

PHILIP   *(putting his head in his hands)* Good grief.

LUCY   *(chuckling)* Welcome to Norfolk!

Lights fade to blackout.

Scene Two

Day One. 15 minutes later. Lights up on empty stage. Lucy and Philip enter holding a mug of tea each.

LUCY   So, have you got all that then, Philip?

PHILIP   I think so.

LUCY   Tea; coffee; kettle; fridge and toilet.

PHILIP   Yes. Although I do think I should get that lock fixed on that toilet door.

LUCY   Really? It doesn't bother me.

PHILIP   Well...

LUCY   *(chuckling)* I mean I'm sure I haven't got anything you've never seen before!

PHILIP   Well...

LUCY   Oh, God. I'm sorry. For all I know you could be gay. You know, this day and age. In which case I possibly have got something you've never seen before! *(She laughs nervously)*

PHILIP   It's fine, Lucy. I'm not gay. I used to be married, to a woman, and I have two children.

LUCY   *(taking her seat)* Ah, good. Well, I don't mean good, because that might suggest I'm homophobic or something... which I'm not... what I mean is... oh dear, I seem to be making a mess of this.

PHILIP   *(taking his seat)* It's alright. I know what you mean.

LUCY   Good! Well I'm glad someone does! *(Pause)* You just have to be so careful these days. So easy to appear to have some sort of phobia or something. So difficult to be 'pc' all the time. I'm very much of the opinion that

43

if you can't spell it, you can't be it! So, there's no way I can be homophobic because I can't spell it!

PHILIP   But you can spell heterosexual? *(He takes a gulp of tea)*

LUCY   Erm, ah, right. I see what you did there… no, I don't think I can spell that either; *(staring at Philip)* but I'm very good at mime.

Philip spits his tea back into his mug.

PHILIP   *(wiping his chin)* Sorry about that!

LUCY   *(getting a tissue from her bag and handing it to Phillip)* No need to be sorry. All my fault.

PHILIP   *(accepting the tissue)* Thank you.

LUCY   And, as you can see, no phone calls whilst we were out in the kitchen.

PHILIP   Yes. Quite amazing. Have you checked if there were any messages on the answerphone from last night?

LUCY   Oh yes. I always do that first thing.

PHILIP   And?

LUCY   Nothing.

PHILIP   Oh. Have you ever had any messages in the four months you've been going?

LUCY   Yes. Three.

PHILIP   Three!? That's all?

LUCY   Do you want to hear about them?

PHILIP   Well; shouldn't really. Client confidentiality and all that.

LUCY	Trust me, I can share them.
PHILIP	Ok.
LUCY	Well. First one was a heavy breather. You know the sort.
PHILIP	Yes.
LUCY	You've had some of them before; in Watford?
PHILIP	Yes. One or two.
LUCY	Anyway, this one was breathing heavy for quite a while, until he realised it was just an answerphone. Then he hung up.
PHILIP	Right.
LUCY	The next one left a message asking for a 17, a 23, a 39 and a portion of chips. *(Laughing)* So, he went hungry that night.
PHILIP	*(laughing)* Ok.
LUCY	And the third one was a lady who'd lost her cat. She left her number, so I phoned her back the next day and gave her the number of the local RSPCA.
PHILIP	I see. At least she got the 'lost' bit of Lost and Found.
LUCY	Yes. I seem to pass the RSPCA phone number onto a lot of people who have got the 'lost' bit.
PHILIP	I see.
LUCY	They don't read beyond the headline around here. *(Retrieving a poster from her desk and reading from it)* 'Lost and Found. If you've lost anything in your life – husband; wife; partner; parent; child, or any loved one – or you're losing someone due to mental health issues; please call us so we can help you find your best way to

45

recover and move on. If you feel lost; don't worry. You've found us.'

PHILIP   *(holding his hand out)* May I see it?

LUCY   *(handing the poster over)* Sure. Didn't you have them in Watford?

PHILIP   Oh, yes. But word of mouth was all we really relied on down there.

LUCY   Yes. Not enough people in Norfolk to rely on word of mouth. Unless everyone owns a loud hailer!

They both laugh.

PHILIP   Have you put many of these up?

LUCY   Oh, just around town.

PHILIP   Ok, well, can I take this and make some copies?

LUCY   Of course.

PHILIP   Then when I find myself in other towns, or even in Norwich, I'll put some up and see if we can spread the word and make our time here a little more worthwhile. Sound ok?

LUCY   Sure.

The phone rings.

LUCY   Blimey! Two in one morning! *(Looking at Philip)* Do you want to take this one?

PHILIP   Oh, yes. Can do. *(He puts the headset on and looks at the keyboard)* Looks the same setup as Watford. This button here?

LUCY   Yes. That's the one.

46

PHILIP	*(pressing the button)* Hello; Lost and Found. My name's Philip, how can I be of assistance? Ah, I see... you've lost who...? Ah, Terrence. I see... well I'm so sorry to hear that... was it sudden...? One minute he was there... and then he'd gone... it can happen like that... yes... when was this...? Yesterday... oh dear... oh dear, oh dear.... You were out for a walk and he just went... oh, dear... *(Philip and Lucy exchange smiles)* and you what...? You want him back...? Well, yes, that's only natural... so, would I be able to what? Look for him? *(Looking at Lucy)* Erm... hang on a minute, er, Mrs Burrows, I just need to have a quick word with my colleague. *(Cupping the microphone. To Lucy)* She lost her husband yesterday and wants us to look for him!
LUCY	Did she say husband?
PHILIP	Well, no, I suppose she didn't.
LUCY	From this end of the conversation it sounded like her dog which ran away yesterday. Whilst she was out on a walk.
PHILIP	Really?
LUCY	Yes. I told you I get a lot of lost animals.
PHILIP	Oh. This is all new to me. I've only ever dealt with people who'd lost people in Watford. Not people who'd lost animals. It's a whole different kettle of fish.
LUCY	Do you want me to take over?
PHILIP	If you don't mind.
LUCY	Pass her over to me then.
PHILIP	*(back into phone)* Sorry about that, Mrs Burrows. I'm just going to pass you onto my colleague, Lucy. She's in a better position to help you... no problem... you're welcome.

LUCY	*(pressing a couple of buttons and speaking into her headset)* Good morning, Mrs Burrows. Philip has told me that you lost Terrence yesterday whilst out walking. I'm sorry to hear that. What exactly happened...? Right... he saw a squirrel and shot off after it... *(she glances over at Philip, who puts his head in his hands)* he's a red setter... right, well the best thing to do is call the local RSPCA. I have their number here. It's 03030401565... is that helpful...? Good.... You're welcome... I hope you find him... bye, bye, now... bye, bye.

They both take their headsets off and burst into laughter.

PHILIP	Oh dear. I thought you were joking when you said you get a lot of lost animals.
LUCY	No. Deadly serious!
PHILIP	I can see that now! I'll get onto spreading these posters around as quick as I can. *(Pause)* Now then; do you think we should get a rota going so that we're not both here at the same time?
LUCY	Maybe. If we get busier. But can we work together for a bit first? I'm enjoying the company. If that's ok with you?
PHILIP	Of course it is. *(Looking around)* Is there a caretaker who locks and unlocks this place.
LUCY	Oh, no. I just come and go as I like. I have my own key. *(Rummaging around in her bag)* I got one cut for you, when I received the email about you starting. *(Finding the key and handing it to Philip)*
PHILIP	Oh. Thank you. So, you just come and go?
LUCY	Yes. At the moment.
PHILIP	Right. Well. Another thing different to Watford.

LUCY	Probably. But, normal for Norfolk!
PHILIP	Oh, right.

Pause

LUCY	So, you said you were married. To a woman.
PHILIP	Yes.
LUCY	Divorced?
PHILIP	No, she died a couple of years ago.
LUCY	Oh, no. I'm so sorry.
PHILIP	It's fine.
LUCY	But I'm so nosey and insensitive. Asking you personal questions and then assuming you got divorced.
PHILIP	It's fine. No problem. Good to find out about each other, seeing as we're sort of working together.
LUCY	I guess so.
PHILIP	If it wasn't for my wife's death I wouldn't be here.
LUCY	How come?
PHILIP	It was Lost and Found that guided me through the dark times. Helped me towards the light. That's why I started volunteering myself. To try and give something back.
LUCY	Ah. That's nice.
PHILIP	You?
LUCY	Me? Oh, I was married. Got divorced about eight or nine years ago.

PHILIP	Oh. Sorry to hear that.
LUCY	Well, you see, we couldn't have children.
PHILIP	Oh, I see.
LUCY	And when I say we; I mean we.
PHILIP	Right.
LUCY	We were both firing blanks. If you know what I mean.
PHILIP	Right, yes.
LUCY	Except he insisted on putting the blame entirely on me and left. We got divorced and that's that!
PHILIP	Right. Was that around here?
LUCY	No. Oldham. Didn't you spot my accent?
PHILIP	Well, I didn't think it was a Norfolk one!
LUCY	Ha!
PHILIP	So, what made you move here?
LUCY	Oh, I don't know. Fresh start. Somewhere a long way from him!
PHILIP	Right. Makes sense, I guess.
LUCY	And I saw an advert for this place opening and thought I'd give it a go.
PHILIP	So you don't do any paid work then?
LUCY	No. No need. Divorce settlement set me up alright.
PHILIP	I see.
LUCY	Do you do any paid work?

PHILIP	I did, in Watford, boring office work. I'm taking a break at the moment. Just settling into the country life!
LUCY	Well; if you ask me, you can't beat it!
PHILIP	I tell you what. Rather than us both sitting here twiddling our thumbs, why don't I pop home, print some copies of this poster off and go for a little drive? See if I can find some notice boards outside village halls and so on. Get spreading the word right now?
LUCY	If you want to, Philip. It's up to you.
PHILIP	*(rising)* Yes. I'll do that and see you tomorrow morning.
LUCY	Ok. I'll see you then.
PHILIP	*(giving a little wave as he exits)* Bye.
LUCY	*(returning the wave)* Yes. Bye for now.

Lucy returns to her bag of Hula Hoops which has remained on her desk throughout. She takes out one Hula Hoop and pushes it on as far as she can onto her wedding ring finger.

There we go. That'll do. *(Looking off to the exit and then back at her new wedding ring)* I now pronounce you Lucy and Philip. You may now kiss in the Wendy House. *(She gives a small laugh. Possibly slightly sinister?)*

Lights fade to blackout.

Scene Three

Day Two. The same, the following morning. Lucy is sat at her desk. She presses a button on her computer. A computer voice responds, 'you have no messages.'

LUCY   Well, there's a surprise! *(She starts to ferret around in her bag and finds a Flake. She holds it for a while, seemingly in a dream, and then unwraps it slowly whilst humming the music from the Flake advert. She then holds it up and starts singing)* Only the crumbliest, flakiest chocolate. Tastes like chocolate's never tasted before. *(She then licks one side of the Flake in a suggestive manner before taking a very large bite.)* Mmmm.

With chocolate crumbling from her mouth, Philip enters. He's holding a folded-up OS map under his arm and he pauses a second to try and take in the situation before proceeding to his desk.

PHILIP   *(jovially)* Morning!

LUCY   *(trying not to gag)* Morning! *(She quickly fumbles in her bag for tissues and wet wipes and starts to wipe her mouth, fingers and desk.)*

PHILIP   Breakfast?

LUCY   *(still tidying up)* Sort of. Sometimes just have an urge.

PHILIP   Fair enough.

LUCY   Do you ever have an urge, Philip?

PHILIP   Yes, I suppose I do. It doesn't usually involve chocolate, though!

LUCY   *(chuckling)* No? *(suggestively)* Not all of mine involve chocolate, either!

PHILIP   *(moving on)* No. In fact, my latest urge was to get as many posters out there as possible. So, I made lots of copies at home and went for that drive. *(Unfolding the map)* Because I haven't lived here very long, I can't remember the names of all the towns and villages I went to, so I brought this map.

LUCY   *(looking at the map)* Blimey!

PHILIP   *(pointing at the map)* So, this is us. I went to there... one poster in the library and one in the supermarket.

LUCY   Right.

PHILIP   Village hall there... public notice board there... council offices there.... College... then places there, there and there.

LUCY   Wow. You have been busy!

PHILIP   Just a start really.

LUCY   Certainly is.

PHILIP   Any messages overnight?

LUCY   No.

PHILIP   Oh, well. Maybe it'll take time. Cup of tea?

LUCY   Oh, yes please, Philip. That'll be lovely!

PHILIP   *(heading to the kitchen)* Milk and one sweetener; right?

LUCY   Yes. Lovely. *(Pause. Calling to the kitchen)* This is the first time I've had a cup of tea made for me since I've volunteered here. Thank you!

PHILIP   *(off. Calling)* I'll try and make it a good one, then.

Lucy laughs and the phone rings.

LUCY   My God! The phone! Philip!

Philip rushes in without the teas and gives Lucy a big thumbs up. Lucy returns the gesture.

LUCY   *(answering the call)* Hello; Lost and Found. My name's Lucy, how can I be of assistance? I see… of course…. Before we continue, can I just ask where you got our number from...? On the notice board outside your village hall? *(She turns and gives another thumbs up to Philip, who exits to finish making the tea. Back into phone)* Thank you. Please continue…. You lost your wife when…?

It is clearly a conversation which is very one-sided at this point with Lucy only saying the occasional 'yes', or 'uh-huh'. Philip returns with the teas. Places one by Lucy, who smiles, and he sits at his desk with his own. After a short while his phone rings. Lucy and Philip share shocked looks.

PHILIP   *(answering the call)* Hello; Lost and Found. My name's Philip, how can I be of assistance? Right… Mrs Roberts, did you say...? Right… I'm so sorry to hear that. When did you lose your husband…? Right…

The respective conversations continue for a short while with the odd 'yes' etc. Lucy and Philip gradually turn their backs towards each other as they become absorbed and wish to make the calls as private and as confidential as they can.

LUCY   And how long had she been under the doctor?

PHILIP   Three months.

LUCY   All that time?

PHILIP   Yes, I can imagine it was claustrophobic.

LUCY   And she felt like he was doing his best?

PHILIP   It's good to hear he kept it up until the end.

LUCY   There're not enough hours in the day.

Pause

PHILIP	Yes, they shrivel up so quickly.
LUCY	GP's are so overstretched these days.
PHILIP	And then there's nothing left. I know.
LUCY	And it was during this that it exploded?
PHILIP	Leaving an empty sack... yes.
LUCY	Sounds messy.
PHILIP	Yes. *(Slight pause)* How did the tattoo affect things?
LUCY	Did this happen at home, or in hospital?
PHILIP	Where was the tattoo?
LUCY	In the park!?
PHILIP	Sorry; whereabouts?
LUCY	Near the ornate lamppost by the swings.
PHILIP	Gosh. That must have hurt!
LUCY	It was one of her favourite places.
PHILIP	Yes; that's understandable. No wonder he had an aversion to needles...
LUCY	Yes. I do like the swings.
PHILIP	Made it difficult to get the drip in...
LUCY	There's nothing better than a good swing!
PHILIP	He had to look away...
LUCY	Although I do enjoy a good see-saw...
PHILIP	Yes; I can imagine that it was difficult to get in...

LUCY	Up…
PHILIP	Lots of prodding.
LUCY	And down.
PHILIP	Again…
LUCY	Up…
PHILIP	And again.
LUCY	And down.
PHILIP	Sounds exhausting.
LUCY	*(chuckling)* And then a quick go on the slide!
PHILIP	Has to be done, doesn't it?

Pause. A few more 'uh-huhs' from both.

LUCY	Time to move on then?
PHILIP	Yes. That's right.
LUCY	Small steps.
PHILIP	Get back on that bike.
LUCY	Best foot forward.
PHILIP	Positive thinking.
LUCY	We're always here.
PHILIP	Anytime.
LUCY	Bye, bye, now.
PHILIP	Goodbye.

They hang up simultaneously and smile at each other.

PHILIP   Well. There we go! It looks like the posters are working straight away!

LUCY   Yes. Not only two calls at once, but no lost animals!

They both laugh.

This calls for a celebration!

PHILIP   *(rising)* Another cuppa?

LUCY   Well, a top-up would be nice. But I was thinking of something stronger.

PHILIP   *(glancing at his watch)* What, at 9:20 in the morning!?

LUCY   What? No, no! Not now! I mean; chocolate at this time of day is bad enough. I don't want you thinking I drink at this time too!

PHILIP   Oh, right.

LUCY   No, I mean later. After we've put in a shift here. Find a pub, or something.

PHILIP   Erm...

LUCY   Maybe have a spot to eat. You know. Up to you.

PHILIP   Erm, well, maybe at some point, Lucy, but I haven't been out with anyone since my wife, you know...

LUCY   What? Oh, I see. I wasn't meaning anything untoward. Just a drink.

PHILIP   Oh, I know that. But, well, you know... best to make things clear from the start.

LUCY   *(slightly put out)* Yes; sure. Fine.

PHILIP (*picking up the mugs and exiting*) But I'll get you that celebratory top-up, and I'll bring in the packet of Hob Nobs.

LUCY Lovely! *(To herself)* Hob Nobs. You're gonna have to up your game, Lucy, or Hob Nobs will be the only knob you get!

Lights fade to blackout.

Scene Four

Day Three. Next morning. Stage is empty. A moment, and Philip enters carrying a packet of Hob Nobs.

PHILIP   Mor... *(realising Lucy isn't there)* Oh! *(He checks his watch)* She's normally here by now. I'll pop these biscuits in the kitchen. Never seen anyone devour Hob Nobs as quick as her.

He exits to the kitchen. He promptly returns, takes his seat and puts his headset on. A moment, then the phone rings.

Ah! *(Into headset)* Hello; Lost and Found. My name's Philip, how can I be of assistance? Right... you went out last night... up the city... right... and this morning you've discovered you've lost what...? Your underwear... Ah, right, well that's not really what we're here for... no... what are we here for? Well, with all due respect, we're here for more important things than lost underwear.... You have lost something more important than your underwear...? Ok... sorry, what was that...? In the process of losing your underwear you think you lost your virginity as well...! Well, yes, that is more important, true, but I'm not sure I can really help... I can? How...? You want to what...? Lose it again, with me? Well, you see, strictly speaking you can only lose it once you see... No, I'm sure you're very pretty, but... hello... hello?

Philip presses a button, takes off his headset and slumps back into his chair. He runs his fingers through his hair and fans himself with one hand.

PHILIP   Bloody hell! Is that normal for Norfolk!?

The phone rings again.

God! I hope it's not her again! *(Into headset)* Hello; Lost and Found. My name's Philip, how can I be of assistance? Yes... ah, right... you've lost your what...? Your pussy... you mean your cat...? Yes... well I can give you the number of the RSPCA... yes, they'll help you find your pu... *(clearing his throat)* cat... yes, cat. Sorry... you miss stroking it... yes, well *(getting*

59

slightly flustered) I have the number here
somewhere.... It's a sphynx cat... oh, no I haven't
heard of that breed... it's a what...? A bald pu *(clearing
his throat again)* cat... right... no... yes... no, I haven't
seen one, erm, well, yes, I guess I would like to see
yours... if you find it.... Ah, here it is
03030401565........... You're welcome... Good luck!
*(he presses a button, takes off his headset and slumps
once more).*

A moment, then Lucy enters.

LUCY	Morning! Everything alright?
PHILIP	*(trying to regather himself)* Morning. Oh, yes, fine. You?
LUCY	Fine, thank you. *(Holding up a packet of Hob Nobs and exiting to the kitchen)* Just stopped off for another packet of these, seeing as you devoured that other packet so rapidly yesterday!
PHILIP	*(to himself)* Me! *(Calling)* Oh; I did the same.
LUCY	*(Calling)* Oh, yes, so you did! Great minds think alike!
PHILIP	*(Calling)* Yes.
LUCY	*(returning and taking her seat)* I've popped the kettle on. Any answerphone messages?
PHILIP	Oh, I haven't checked yet.
LUCY	Right; let's see. *(She presses a button and hears 'you have no messages')* Oh, well! Any calls before I came in?
PHILIP	*(slightly flustered)* Erm, yes, funnily enough, a couple.
LUCY	Two? Already? Great. Anything you're able to discuss with me?
PHILIP	Erm, well, actually they were a bit more of the type you used to get.

LUCY	What do you mean?
PHILIP	Erm, well, one lady had lost her *(he gives a slight cough to clear his throat)* cat and the other had lost her virg… I mean, lost something on a Virgin train.
LUCY	Oh, right.
PHILIP	So, I passed the correct phone numbers on to them.
LUCY	Right, lovely. *(Rising)* The kettle must be boiled. I'll get that cuppa. *(She exits)*

A moment, then the phone rings.

PHILIP *(he looks after Lucy, realises he'd better take it, puts on his headphones and answers)* Hello; Lost and Found. My name's Philip, how can I be of assistance...? Who's lost...? You are...? Well, that's not really what we're here for… Where...? You're lost in France…. How did you find our number…? *(he looks around for Lucy to no avail)* In the fields the birds are singing… that's nice, but I think you need the police… You're lost in France… yes, you've already said that… try 999 or… sorry? The day's just beginning… yes… although, strictly speaking, you're an hour ahead of us… try neuf, neuf, neuf…. You're what...? Standing there in the morning rain…. You've got a feeling you can't explain…. You're lost in France… yes, I've got that bit… and you're what…? In love… that's nice… but… hello, hello… *(he hangs up, looks around, ponders a bit and suddenly picks up a pen and piece of paper. He writes as he speaks)* I was lost in France, in the fields the birds were singing. I was lost in France, and the day was just beginning. As I stood there in the morning rain, I had a feeling I can't explain. I was lost in France, in love. *(He pauses and re-reads it to himself)* Bloody hell! That's a Bonnie Tyler song! *(Pause whilst taking in the lyrics again)* Who the hell phones a helpline and quotes Bonnie Tyler?

Lucy returns with the teas and Hob Nobs which she's transferred into a box.

61

LUCY	*(handing Philip his tea and sitting)* Everything alright? Did I hear the phone?
PHILIP	*(scratching his head)* Er, yes, you did. Very bizarre.
LUCY	Really. Why's that?
PHILIP	This woman made out she was lost in France, and required help, but she ended up quoting lyrics from the song Lost in France by Bonnie Tyler!
LUCY	*(laughing)* That certainly is very bizarre! *(She opens the box of biscuits and offers them to Philip)* Maybe she's Holding Out For a Hero? *(she fixes Philip with a stare)*
PHILIP	*(taking a biscuit)* Maybe.
LUCY	Or she's possibly having A Total Eclipse of the Heart?
PHILIP	*(laughing)* Yes, possibly. *(He takes a bite of the biscuit)* Oh.
LUCY	Alright?
PHILIP	Yes, just this biscuit tastes a bit different.
LUCY	Really? *(She takes a bite of her own biscuit)* Mine tastes fine.
PHILIP	Oh. Mine tastes a bit salty. What is it?
LUCY	Just a Hob Nob. I emptied the two packets into this box.
PHILIP	Oh.
LUCY	Dunk it in your tea. That'll probably help.
PHILIP	Yes, right. *(He does so)* Yes, that's a little better.
LUCY	*(rising)* Good! I'm just popping to the loo. *(She exits)*
PHILIP	Right. *(Philip watches her leave. He then sniffs the remainder of his biscuit, shakes his head and places it in his jacket pocket)*

The phone rings.

PHILIP   *(into headset)* Hello; Lost and Found. My name's Philip, how can I be of assistance? Hello… hello… hello, can I help you…? *(hanging up)* Great. Heavy breather now.

Lucy re-enters putting her mobile in her pocket.

LUCY   *(taking her seat)* You alright, Philip?

PHILIP   On top of cats, virgin… trains and Bonnie Tyler, I've just had a heavy breather!

LUCY   Oh dear. Maybe the posters have just attracted all the weird and wonderful of Norfolk. Rather than the needy.

PHILIP   It seems that way.

LUCY   Have you checked the numbers against each other? To see if they're different people or just one person mucking us about?

PHILIP   *(looking at the screen)* They're all different numbers and I could hear they were different people.

LUCY   Oh, well. Just a weird morning then!

PHILIP   Must be. Yes.

The phone rings. Lucy and Philip look at each other.

LUCY   Do you want me to take this one?

PHILIP   Yes, please. If you don't mind.

LUCY   Ok. *(Answering the phone)* Hello; Lost and Found. My name's Lucy, how can I be of assistance...? Yes… that's right… oh dear… and are you getting help from the hospice…? *(she smiles at Philip who offers a shrug in return)* You just want someone to talk to? Well, that's what I'm here for…

This conversation continues with Lucy mostly listening. Philip rises, picks up his mug of tea and makes a gesture towards Lucy offering to refill her

63

mug. She nods and hands him her mug. He takes both mugs in one hand, walks up stage, takes the biscuit from his jacket pocket, gives it another sniff, shakes his head and replaces it in his pocket. He exits as

Lights fade to blackout.

Scene Five

Day Four. Next morning. The same. Lucy enters humming the tune, or possibly even singing the words, to 'Lost in France' by Bonnie Tyler. She's carrying a Tupperware box of homemade biscuits which she places on Philip's desk. She exits to the kitchen. A moment, then Philip enters. He proceeds to his desk and eyes the Tupperware box with caution. He sits and presses a button. 'You have no messages' is heard.

LUCY	*(returning from the kitchen)* Morning, Philip.
PHILIP	*(looking up)* Oh, morning, Lucy.
LUCY	*(Pointing at the box)* I made you some chocolate brownies last night. I hope you like them.
PHILIP	Oh, lovely, thank you.
LUCY	*(sitting)* I've only been here a few minutes. Have you checked if there are any answerphone messages?
PHILIP	Yes, just now. Nothing.
LUCY	Oh, dear. Never mind. Although I suppose that's good.
PHILIP	What is?
LUCY	No calls. No calls means no one is in need.
PHILIP	I see what you mean, Lucy. But Lost and Found know that people are in need; all over the country. That's why they came into existence.
LUCY	I know that, Philip.
PHILIP	And it can't just be Norfolk people that can cope with everything thrown at them without the occasional bit of help and support.
LUCY	Well; I've lived here longer than you, Philip, and I have to say that generally they are a breed apart!
PHILIP	That's as maybe; but I still think we need to market ourselves more. Get more posters out there to spread the word.

LUCY	But, you've already put all those posters up the other day.
PHILIP	Yes; I put them up. But someone else has taken them down!
LUCY	*(reacting with surprise)* You what?
PHILIP	Well, after the number of calls dwindled again yesterday, I took the scenic route home and discovered about 90% of the posters I'd put up had been removed.
LUCY	Well I never.
PHILIP	A little strange, wouldn't you say?
LUCY	I would. Who do you think did that? The council?
PHILIP	No. Lost and Found have clearance to do random posting.
LUCY	Oh. *(Giving it some thought)* Maybe they were taken down by a not-so-good Samaritan?
PHILIP	I beg your pardon?
LUCY	Well, I don't know, maybe the Samaritans thought we were wrestling in on their market.
PHILIP	I'm not really sure that that's a trait of the Samaritans.
LUCY	Maybe not. *(Moving on)* Have a brownie. It'll cheer you up!
PHILIP	It's a bit early for me, Lucy.
LUCY	*(opening the box and offering)* Nonsense. I made them especially for you. Go on.
PHILIP	*(reluctantly taking one)* Ok. Just the one. *(He takes a small bite)*
LUCY	Nice?
PHILIP	Yes, lovely. Thank you, Lucy.

LUCY	Not too salty?
PHILIP	Salty?
LUCY	Yes. Like the Hob Nob you tried yesterday.
PHILIP	Oh, no. Absolutely fine.
LUCY	*(rising)* Excellent. I'll go and make you a tea to go with that. *(She exits to the kitchen)*
PHILIP	*(calling)* Thank you! *(Looking at the cake; to himself whilst removing a small plastic bag from his pocket)* And as for you! *(He places the remaining piece of brownie in the bag and puts it in his jacket pocket)* And cue phone!

The phone rings on cue.

	(to himself) Very sloppy. Very predictable. How you got away with everything for this long. *(Answering the phone)* Hello; Lost and Found. My name's Philip, how can I be of assistance...? Hello... hello...? Do you have asthma...? Are you returning home from a night out at a Star Wars convention where you went as Darth Vader...? Oh... *(he hangs up by pressing a button and takes his headset off)*
LUCY	*(returning from the kitchen with mugs of tea)* Everything alright? That was the phone, wasn't it?
PHILIP	Yes.
LUCY	Anything interesting?
PHILIP	Just a heavy breather, again.
LUCY	Oh, dear. Not having much luck, are we?
PHILIP	It would seem that way.
LUCY	*(she puts Philip's tea on his desk and takes her seat)* Never mind.

PHILIP	*(rising)* Look, Lucy, I think I need to get out there and put more posters up.
LUCY	Really? Now? You've only just got here.
PHILIP	I know. But I do find it very frustrating just sitting here twiddling my thumbs when people might need our help.
LUCY	You don't have to just twiddle your thumbs. *(Rising and getting closer to Philip)* We could have a nice chat.
PHILIP	True. But I think I need to do this first. If that's ok?
LUCY	*(slightly disgruntled)* If that's what you want.
PHILIP	Thank you.
LUCY	You could at least stay and finish your tea, couldn't you?
PHILIP	I think I need to do this *(picking up his tea and taking a quick swig)* first. But, thank you for the tea, Lucy. *(He eyes the box of cakes)* Can I take these with me?
LUCY	*(slightly taken aback)* Yes, of course. You liked it that much?
PHILIP	*(taking the box)* Oh, yes. Delicious!
LUCY	*(smiling)* Lovely!
PHILIP	Great! *(He gives Lucy a quick kiss on her cheek)* Thank you. I'll probably be back sometime this afternoon.
LUCY	I'll look forward to it!
PHILIP	*(as he exits)* Bye.
LUCY	Bye, Philip. Take care. *(She sits down at her desk. In a lower tone)* You'll have to take care if you eat too many of those brownies. *(She gives a little evil laugh as she rises again and picks up the two mugs)* Come to mummy, Philip. Come to mummy. *(She heads towards the kitchen singing Total Eclipse of the Heart by Bonnie Tyler)* Turn around, every now and then I get a

little bit lonely and you're never coming round... *(she stops before exiting)* Except you are coming round now, Philip, aren't you!? *(She exits to the kitchen.)*

Lights fade to blackout.

Scene Six

Day Four. Later that afternoon. Lucy is sitting at her desk whilst taking Jelly Babies out of a bag and lining them on her desk whilst singing 'Oranges and Lemons.'

LUCY   *(singing)* Oranges and lemons, say the bells of St Clements. You owe me five farthings, say the bells of St Martins. When will you pay me? Say the bells of Old Bailey. When I grow rich, say the bells of Shoreditch. When will that be? Say the bells of Stepney. I do not know, says the great bell of Bow. Here comes a candle to light you to bed and here comes a chopper to chop off your head. *(Throughout the next Lucy violently brings her hand down in a chopping action to chop off the heads of the jelly babies; or at least squash them)* Chop, chop, chop, chop. The last one is dead!

Lucy surveys the carnage all over her desk. She picks up one squashed Jelly Baby, smiles, and pops it in her mouth. A moment and Philip enters. He's holding the Tupperware box which appears to be empty. He's swaying slightly and holding his head.

         (noticing Philip, she rises and goes to steady him) Oh, Philip. Are you alright? You don't look too good.

PHILIP   *(still swaying)* I don't feel too good. I think I need to sit down.

Lucy grabs Philip's chair and brings it closer to him so he can sit down.

LUCY   There you go.

PHILIP   *(sitting)* Thank you.

LUCY   *(seeing the empty box she takes it from Philip and opens it)* My God, Philip! Have you eaten all of these?

PHILIP   *(drowsily)* Erm, yes, I guess I must have.

LUCY   But there was a dozen in there. I can't believe you've managed to eat them all and remain standing.

PHILIP   I'm not standing.

LUCY	No, quite. I can't believe you're with me at all. You should be in a coma.
PHILIP	Should I?
LUCY	*(kneeling next to him and feeling his chest and arms)* I thought you'd be a big, strong one to knock out. I didn't think you'd survive twelve of those brownies, plus the tea this morning. Not that you actually drank much of that.
PHILIP	*(appearing to lose consciousness)* What are you saying?
LUCY	Well, I suppose there's no harm in explaining, you'll probably be gone by the time I finish.
PHILIP	Gone? Gone where?
LUCY	Just you close your eyes and let my voice be the last thing you hear.

Philip closes his eyes and slumps slightly.

That's it. Now then. You're my third here, you know. Three in Lancashire and now three in Norfolk. Probably time to move on after you, although this set up here at Lost and Found is quite convenient. You're the third man to have come in here having lost their wife, looking to help others. It's all too easy. *(She gets her chair and pulls it next to Philip's)* It was my husband who started it. Beating me up because I couldn't conceive. Or in his words, wouldn't conceive. He was firing blanks, but it was my fault, according to him. Broke three of my ribs one time, throwing me down the stairs. We eventually got divorced, but he still kept on at me so, one evening, I decided to push him back. He tripped on the hearth rug and cracked his head on the marble fireplace. Gone. Just like that. The thrill I got was amazing. What a buzz. All those years I'd cowed away from him; from all men, but I suddenly discovered I was strong enough to beat them. To destroy men. The worm; this worm, had turned. *(Pause. She goes over to her desk and pops a Jelly Baby in her mouth before returning to her seat)* When we'd

71

divorced, he'd left a pond at the end of the garden unfinished. So, I dragged him down there, dug down a bit further and buried him. I then covered him with the pond liner and filled the pond with water. Job done. *(She gets another Jelly Baby and returns. She gives Philip a little shove. He groans)* Blimey, still with us? I'll keep going then. So, I then tried to get a new man. Not because I needed one; but because I had found this new urge to be the dominant one in a relationship. But it was hard work. It took so long and I could never make any headway. So, I thought, sod this, let's have some fun! I got some Rohypnol; you know, the date rape drug, and tried it on this bloke. God it was good but it left him, well, how shall I put it, a bit limp, so I pushed him into the Manchester Ship Canal and started to experiment. Getting the dosage of Rohypnol and Viagra just right took a while, but it was a fun process. The next one in Lancashire was semi-conscious and well, semi everything really so, when I got rid of him, I moved over here. Still with me, Philip? *(a quieter groan this time)* Good. So, I've managed to have fun with two blokes over here. Where are they, you ask – well, you would if you could! – let's just say that lots of houses aren't on the mains sewage system around here; if you get my drift. I have to say that the other two from here were a bit old and weak, but you, Philip, well, you're the one I've been waiting for. *(She starts to rub his chest and slowly moves her hand down)* The Rohypnol has clearly worked. Let's see how the Viagra is getting on.

As Lucy's hand almost reaches Philip's groin, he 'comes to' and swiftly grabs Lucy's wrist with one hand whilst retrieving a pair of handcuffs from his jacket pocket with his other hand. He swiftly cuffs one of Lucy's wrists and attaches the other cuff to one of the chairs. He then stands up and takes a step, or two, away from Lucy so as to make a safe distance between them.

What the!? *(She pulls at the handcuffs, but all it does is make the chair jolt around a bit)*

PHILIP   Is that part of your plan, Lucy? Or should I say Kathy?

LUCY   What!? What are you doing? Who are you?

PHILIP	DI Ben Hargreaves.
LUCY	Show me your badge.
PHILIP	*(laughing)* My badge. You're priceless, you are. I don't carry my badge when I'm working under cover, and you're wearing my cuffs which should really tell you that I'm a police officer.
LUCY	But, all the stuff about your wife dying, and Lost and Found.
PHILIP	Cover story, Kathy, cover story. Now, you sit still whilst I bore you with information. After living in your house in Greater Manchester for almost six years, the couple who you sold it to had a child and decided, for safety reasons, to fill the pond in. During this process the remains of your ex-husband, John, were found buried underneath the pond. And, to cut a long story short, this opened up a trail which, after three years, has brought me here face-to-face with Kathy Williams, or is it Lucy Jenkins?
LUCY	Huh!
PHILIP	Trail of bodies showing Rohypnol and Viagra, in varying degrees, in their bloodstreams. Very interesting. A new one on our coroner. And here you are. Never in the room when I get a crank call here. Owner of several sim cards, to keep the phone numbers changing, and a voice-changing app. You are good. You just got a bit sloppy being so obvious with the phone calls. I have to ask though; what is it with Bonnie Tyler?

The phone rings. They both stare at the computers.

That'll be another crank call. Seeing as you went around everywhere I'd shown you on that map and took down all the posters I'd put up, it can't be anything but a crank call.

The phone continues to ring.

LUCY	Are you answering that, Ben?

PHILIP	Why should I?
LUCY	Why shouldn't you? I'm a bit tied up at the moment!
PHILIP	Right. *(He puts his headset on whilst watching Lucy all the time. Into headset)* Hello. Who's that...? What...? Lucy who!? *(He looks at Lucy who's giving him a slightly manic grin. To Lucy)* What are you doing? Some recorded message or timed device? *(Lucy continues to smile and shrugs. Into headset)* Who is this...? This is DI Hargreaves and I'm putting a trace on this call. *(He starts pressing keys on the keyboard)*
LUCY	I wouldn't do that Detective Inspector.
PHILIP	Do what?
LUCY	Try to trace the call.
PHILIP	You keep out of this. I'm putting an end to your trickery once and for all.
LUCY	Ok. Don't say I didn't warn you.

Philip continues to press keys. Suddenly there's a buzzing noise as it appears that Philip is being electrocuted via the headset, straight into his brain. He holds the headset and screams in agony and slumps to the floor. Lucy leans over and presses a button on the keyboard. The buzzing stops. She coolly reaches into Philip's jacket pocket and retrieves the key for the handcuffs. She uncuffs herself and stands up straight; looking down at Philip.

So, you really want to know what it is about Bonnie Tyler, do you? *(laughing)* Well you know what they say about Bonnie Tyler and Rod Stewart, don't you? *(Pause)* Two different people, apparently. But you never see them in the same room, at the same time! *(She continues to laugh as she pops another Jelly Baby in her mouth. She starts to walk around Philip's body whilst singing 'Do Ya Think I'm Sexy?' by Rod Stewart)* If you want my body and you think I'm sexy, come on sugar let me know. If you really need me just reach out and touch me, come on honey tell me so.

Throughout the above lights fade to blackout.

The End

76

Isolation Stories
Two One-Scene Plays

Ed and Eddie
by
Melissa Collin

FIZZical
by
Ashley Burgoyne

The stage directions were written for these plays to be performed online, in the style of a webcam call. For the stage, the actors can be placed however the director requires, to appear as though they are making video calls.

78

Cast

Edwina (*70s/80s*)
Ruth (*30s/40s, her daughter*)

Ed and Eddie

A small terraced house. Edwina, a woman in her 70/80s talks to the audience as if she is talking into a computer screen. Ruth appears in split screen.

EDWINA   *(peering into the screen)* Look at him! What's he doing now? Honestly, love, If I've told him once I've told him a million times to get rid of that thing.

RUTH   *(looking over her shoulder)* Mum, I'm trying to have a serious...

EDWINA   Just a minute, love... *(shouting)* Ed! Oh, that bloody man.

RUTH   Mum, he can't hear you from there.

EDWINA   It's all very well wanting to feed the birds, but it brings in the cats. And the rats! Dear God... But he won't be told. Stubborn old bugger. You'd think he was David sodding Attenborough.

RUTH   Mother!

EDWINA   Sorry love, but you know how much that garden means to me.

RUTH   I know Mum. But Dad's not doing any harm. It's only a bird feeder.

EDWINA   And is he washing his hands?

RUTH   Of course he is, Mum. Constantly. We both are. My hands are like a ninety year-old's.

EDWINA   Just use some Nivea, love. I bought you some for your birthday, remember?

RUTH   Yes, you did. And I am. It's my nails too. God knows how long it'll be before I can see Mandy.

EDWINA   You've got lovely nails under all that rubbish. I don't know why you bother.

RUTH	Well, I can't bother now, can I? I'll be like a bloody yeti at this rate, too.
EDWINA	You're beautiful. Honestly, why do you young women…
RUTH	I'm hardly young, Mum.
EDWINA	…*young* women do all this? Men aren't bothered about all that.
RUTH	I think you'll find they are.
EDWINA	Your dad never was.
RUTH	Things are different now, Mum.
EDWINA	Not when it comes to some things, they aren't. Not really.
RUTH	You're always, and I mean always, asking me when I'm going to find a man.
EDWINA	I am not!
RUTH	Implying it, then! I have to make the effort. No chance of that at the moment, though. God, I even had a go at cutting my own fringe.
EDWINA	Oh, is that what that is?
RUTH	Very funny. But who the hell is going to see it but Dad?
EDWINA	It's very good of you to be there with him, love.
RUTH	Oh, Mum.
EDWINA	No. I mean it. He's not easy to live with. I know that better than anyone.
RUTH	Mum, I know you wanted to stay.
EDWINA	Yes. I did.

RUTH	You are much better off with Tom and Judy. Oh, don't do the face.
EDWINA	What face?
RUTH	That face. The 'Judy face'. The one you always pull whenever anyone mentions her name.
EDWINA	I do not do a face.
RUTH	You do! It's that face you just pulled. You shouldn't Mum. You know she's very fond of you.
EDWINA	Is she?
RUTH	You know she is. And if she's protective of Tom....
EDWINA	Protective!
RUTH	...it's only because she loves him.
EDWINA	She treats him like a child. He doesn't have a mind of his own anymore.
RUTH	Well you treat Dad like a child.
EDWINA	I have to Ruth.
RUTH	*(pause)* Do you want to speak to him?
EDWINA	I shouldn't. I don't want to leave you to deal with how upset it makes him. You know how confused he is about me not being there.
RUTH	I don't mind dealing with it Mum. He sometimes just calls me Eddie as we chat and he seems happy enough.
EDWINA	Happy enough...
RUTH	Mum...
EDWINA	I don't want him being 'happy enough'. I should be there with him, not here with Tom and that woman.

RUTH	It can't be helped Mum. You know the reasons and we can't do otherwise.
EDWINA	Has he got his medicine?
RUTH	Yes. A very lovely young man came round with his pills. One of the street volunteers. We have several just for this street. They bring round everything we need.
EDWINA	Very nice of him. We've got something similar here, but while Tom can still get out we don't take up their time.
RUTH	There are loads of them. Dad got a little bit upset when the lad called him Edwin. He wasn't to know.
EDWINA	Did he?
RUTH	Poor lad. Dad shouting "It's Ed. Not Edwin. Ed and Eddie. Always has been. Not Edwin and Edwina. Makes us sound like a music hall act." I think he was ok about it. They're all very well-meaning.
EDWINA	Oh, Ruth…
RUTH	It's ok Mum. People see all sorts now. Everyone is very nice and patient. Everyone has to be…
EDWINA	The people with no real worries.
RUTH	That's not fair!
EDWINA	No. I know.
RUTH	Mum. I said I was trying to have a serious conversation with you.
EDWINA	Love; can't it wait?
RUTH	Not really. I think you know what it's about.
EDWINA	Yes.
RUTH	You must've known when you asked me to find the paperwork.

EDWINA	Yes. I suppose I did. But I'm not there and I need the paperwork to make everything right. For you, and Tom. And Dad. Just in case.
RUTH	I know.
EDWINA	So. Go on…
RUTH	I found Tom's birth certificate, and mine. And your marriage licence. But not Dad's divorce papers.
EDWINA	Well, that's no surprise. Sheila probably had them.
RUTH	That's what I thought. But it's your marriage licence, Mum. Dad is listed as a bachelor. But he wasn't, was he?
EDWINA	Ruth…
RUTH	Mum…
EDWINA	Oh, Ruth… don't, love.
RUTH	Mum, was Dad still married when you married him?
EDWINA	Oh, Ruth…
RUTH	God, Mum. He was!
EDWINA	Ruth, you don't understand….
RUTH	No, I bloody don't! What reason could there possibly be to do that?
EDWINA	You like to tell me how different things are now. Well things were certainly different then.
RUTH	Not that much!
EDWINA	Oh, they were. Especially for women. Sheila refused to divorce your dad. Her family were on her side. There was nothing he could do. They were terribly unhappy, Ruth. They had no children. He couldn't stay.
RUTH	And there was you, and Tom.

EDWINA	Yes. He wanted to look after us both, even though Tom wasn't his. We thought we'd just live together at first, even though that wasn't the done thing. He supported Sheila, as well as us. It was hard, Ruth.
RUTH	Yes. I'm sure it was.
EDWINA	Then Sheila went back to Scotland, and apart from the money your dad sent every month, they had no more contact. People assumed they'd got divorced, even your Granny and Grandad. And we let people think that. Lack of money gave us the perfect excuse for a very quiet wedding.
RUTH	Oh Mum… if he'd been found out.
EDWINA	But he wasn't. Then of course, Sheila died a few years later. Ironic, really. We could just have waited!
RUTH	Mum!
EDWINA	Sorry love. I didn't mean that.
RUTH	God Mum. What a mess.
EDWINA	Is it? I don't see how. I should've told you, but I didn't. You know now. It makes no difference really.
RUTH	I suppose not.
EDWINA	I'm sorry love. You had to know sooner or later I suppose.
RUTH	Life is so weird at the moment, this can't make it any more so.
EDWINA	I just want to be back with your dad. That's all I want. I worry I won't see him again. Or that he won't know me.
RUTH	Oh Mum. I will look after him you know. And he will know you.
EDWINA	I know love. We've never been apart like this before. It's all so horrible.

RUTH	Look, Mum, he's coming in from the garden. Are you sure you won't speak to him?
EDWINA	No. It's for the best. Just tell him how much I love him.
RUTH	He knows that, Mum. He always has.
EDWINA	*(smiling)* And get rid of that bloody bird feeder!

Lights fade to blackout.

The End

88

Cast

George *(80s)*
Jemima *(30s/40s, George's daughter*)
Benjamin *(30s/40s, George's son)*

FIZZical

Lights up on a very basic living room with a sideboard and a small dining table with two chairs. Television out of sight. On one of these chairs sits George, 80s. He's staring at a laptop. Behind the laptop is a huge stack of toilet rolls. (This play could just as easily be viewed with the individuals speaking directly into their computer screens, with slight movement of the webcam by George to show the toilet rolls.) George is engaged in an online conversation. We join towards the end of the conversation.

JEMIMA   *(from the laptop)* Now, are sure you've got enough food, Dad?

GEORGE   I've already said that I'm fine, darling.

JEMIMA   Are you sure?

GEORGE   I told you that Mrs Chambers, across the road, got me plenty of bits just a couple of days ago.

JEMIMA   Ok. *(Pause)* Loo rolls?

GEORGE   Sorry?

JEMIMA   Do you have enough loo rolls? I hear there's been a bit of a run on them, so to speak.

GEORGE   *(glancing over the top of the laptop at the huge amount of toilet rolls)* I'll get by.

JEMIMA   Good. *(Pause)* We don't mean to fuss Dad, it's just difficult times and we're all worried about you.

GEORGE   I know you are. But I've managed seventeen years by myself, Jemima. I've spent 95% of my time on my own during those seventeen years. Twelve weeks at 100% won't kill me.

JEMIMA   No it won't, Dad. But this coronavirus will, if you catch it. Particularly at your age and with your lungs.

George chuckles

JEMIMA	*(quite sternly)* Nothing about this is remotely funny, Dad.
GEORGE	'Every bubble's passed its FIZZical!'
JEMIMA	Pardon?
GEORGE	'Every bubble's passed its FIZZical.' *(Pause)* The old advert.
JEMIMA	Old advert for what, Dad?
GEORGE	Corona. The fizzy drink. Do you remember that?
JEMIMA	Not really, Dad.
GEORGE	*(disappointed)* Oh. You used to rush out to the Corona man when he came around in his van. You'd take back the empties and return with the orangeade and the dandelion and burdock and…
JEMIMA	*(interrupting)* Right, well, unfortunately it's not that type of Corona, Dad.
GEORGE	No. Shame. *(Pause)* Could've belched it away if it was…
JEMIMA	*(rushing on)* Quite. Look, I need to get back to work, Dad. Working from home is tricky, particularly with the children needing access to the laptop for schoolwork.
GEORGE	Righto, Jemima. I'll let you get on.
JEMIMA	Thanks, Dad. And remember; it's Jem.
GEORGE	Sorry?
JEMIMA	I haven't been called Jemima for thirty years.
GEORGE	Sorry, darling. Force of habit. *(Pause)* Your mother chose all your names, you know?
JEMIMA	I know, Dad.

GEORGE	So it's just a little link back to her…
JEMIMA	I know, Dad.
GEORGE	…and Jemima's such a pretty name.
JEMIMA	I was named after a duck, Dad.
GEORGE	I know, darling. I couldn't help it that your mum was such an admirer of Beatrix Potter.
JEMIMA	I know. Look, I'm going now. Take care Dad. And get in touch if you need anything. Anything at all.
GEORGE	I will. Send my love to everyone.
JEMIMA	I will do. Bye.
GEORGE	Bye, Jem… *(He presses the button to end the call. To himself)* …ima.

George stands up and takes a square or two of toilet roll and blows his nose. He sits back down for a few seconds and then stands back up and heads for the sideboard. He retrieves a box from the sideboard and returns to his seat at the table. He starts to remove objects from the box, including photos.

GEORGE	*(looking at some photos. To himself)* There you are, Doris. 1954. Beautiful. You always hated your name, didn't you? 'I want my children to have pretty names,' you used to say. 'I'm not going to burden them with stuffy old names, like Doris!' They didn't appreciate it, did they? They all went and shortened them, didn't they?

There's a sound from the laptop denoting an incoming video call. George moves the box to one side and answers the call.

BENJAMIN	*(from the laptop)* Hi, Dad.
GEORGE	Benjamin! How lovely to see you!
BENJAMIN	You too, Dad. You getting to grips with all the video calling?

GEORGE	Come on, Benjamin, you know me. I'm old, not senile.
BENJAMIN	Sorry… so how's everything going?
GEORGE	Fine. You?
BENJAMIN	Well, not good really.
GEORGE	Why? What's happened?
BENJAMIN	Well, now I've had to close the salon, things are getting a bit tight.
GEORGE	Oh dear.
BENJAMIN	And for all the suggestions to work from home, it doesn't work for a hairdresser, does it!?
GEORGE	No, I suppose it doesn't. *(Pause)* Unless…
BENJAMIN	Unless what, Dad?
GEORGE	Well, do you still sell wigs at your salon?
BENJAMIN	Yes. Why?
GEORGE	Well, maybe you could get a customer on video call. Put on a similar wig to your customer. Then you cut the wig and they copy you. It'll be a sort of mirror image, won't it?
BENJAMIN	*(laughing)* Are you serious, Dad?
GEORGE	*(keeping a straight face)* Of course.
BENJAMIN	No. You're having me on!
GEORGE	Would I?
BENJAMIN	Yes!
GEORGE	*(bursting into laughter)* Of course I'm having you on. That's the most ridiculous idea I've ever come up with!
BENJAMIN	God, Dad! You don't improve with age, do you?

GEORGE	Good! I'm determined not to improve with age!
BENJAMIN	*(laughing and spying the box on the table)* What's in the box?
GEORGE	Oh, you know. Just some old memorabilia. *(He starts to remove some items from the box)* War stuff and old photos of your mum. *(He holds up a picture of Doris to the camera)*
BENJAMIN	Is that Mum?
GEORGE	Yes.
BENJAMIN	She looks like Jem in that one.
GEORGE	*(looking at the photo)* Yes. I suppose she does.
BENJAMIN	Looking for the old Blitz Spirit to help you through the pandemic, eh Dad?
GEORGE	*(removing a child's gas mask from the box)* Well, if I could survive the Second World War, I can survive this!
BENJAMIN	You were only a child, Dad.
GEORGE	No matter. I still survived.
BENJAMIN	*(pause)* Was that your gas mask?
GEORGE	*(holding up the gas mask)* Yes. This went everywhere with me during the war.
BENJAMIN	Shame it's a child's one. Might be handy against the virus.
GEORGE	*(chuckling as he places the gas mask back down)* Yes. *(Pause)* Have you heard from your brother?
BENJAMIN	No, not since last week.
GEORGE	Poor Jeremy. He must be snowed under at the hospital.
BENJAMIN	It's not good, Dad.

GEORGE	No, it's not.
BENJAMIN	But Jez'll be fine. He always is.
GEORGE	Yes. I suppose he always is.

Pause

BENJAMIN	Right; better go.
GEORGE	Ok, son. Speak soon.
BENJAMIN	Yes… Ah, just remembered. We've done an online shopping order for you.
GEORGE	Have you? That's very kind of you Benjamin, but I'm alright for things at the moment.
BENJAMIN	Well it won't be coming for three weeks, so you're bound to be needing things by then.
GEORGE	Well, yes. I suppose I will.
BENJAMIN	Just the basics, you know… bread, milk, etc.
GEORGE	Lovely. Thank you.
BENJAMIN	No problem. Oh, and a pack of eighteen loo rolls. You'll probably be short of them in three weeks' time.
GEORGE	*(glancing once more over the laptop at the mountain of toilet rolls)* Possibly.
BENJAMIN	Right. I'll be in touch soon. Stay safe.
GEORGE	You too, Benjamin. Bye.
BENJAMIN	Bye.

The call is ended. George starts to put things back in the box. He leaves the gas mask until last.

GEORGE *(to himself)* Jez… Jem… At least he didn't tell me off for calling him Benjamin! *(He addresses a photo of Doris)* With all these name changes we might as well have just called them Flopsy, Mopsy and Cottontail! *(He picks up the gas mask and sits in the armchair. Looking at the gas mask)* Coronavirus. 'Every bubble's passed its FIZZical.'

George smiles and picks up the remote for his TV and turns it on. A news channel starts up. The subject matter is the coronavirus. He hops through some channels. They're all equally as depressing. He turns off the TV and looks once more at the child size gas mask.

'Every bubble's passed its FIZZical.'

George chuckles as he decides to put on the gas mask. As it's a child's gas mask, it's very tight and looks silly. He leans back in his chair with the gas mask on.

Lights fade to blackout.

The End

Printed in Great Britain
by Amazon